PARANORMAL IN THE ~~WESTCO~~
Michael Williams

Bossiney Books

First published in 1986
by Bossiney Books
St Teath, Bodmin, Cornwall.
Printed and bound in Great Britain by
A. Wheaton & Co. Ltd, Exeter.

PLATE ACKNOWLEDGMENTS

Front cover by Mark Bygrave
Ray Bishop: pages 4, 7, 12, 22, 35, 41, 51, 57, 59,
    67, 76, 78, 82, 86, 92 and back cover
Felicity Young: pages 43, 44, 45, 60
Rosemary Clinch: pages 5, 26
Michael Clinch: pages 19, 25
Marylou North: pages 8, 47
Julia Davey: pages 36, 81
Richard Isbell: page 9
Fay Godwin: page 11
Michael Deering: page 13
Alice Boyd: page 15
David C. Golby: pages 31, 32
Roy Westlake: page 38
Paul Broadhurst: page 54
Acora: page 63
Barbara Hicken: page 64
David Clarke: page 73
Richard W. Hawken: page 91

About the Author and the Book

A Cornishman, Michael Williams started full-time publishing in 1975. With his wife Sonia, he runs Bossiney Books from a cottage and converted barn in North Cornwall – they are literally cottage publishers, specialising in Westcountry subjects by Westcountry authors. For ten years they ran the Bossiney House Hotel, just outside Tintagel – hence the name Bossiney Books.

Outside publishing and writing, Michael Williams is a keen cricket enthusiast and collector of cricket books. He is President of the Cornish Crusaders Cricket Club and a member of the Cornwall and Gloucestershire County Clubs. He is also a member of the RSPCA, and has actively worked for reform in laws relating to animal welfare. In 1984, he was elected to the Ghost Club, and remains convinced Cornwall is the most haunted area in the whole of Great Britain.

In *Paranormal in the Westcountry* Michael Williams explores a whole range of areas 'beyond normal explanation'. Ghost hunting and healing, psychic painting and tarot cards, mediumship and psycho-expansion, *I Ching* and astrology are all featured – and nearly all the photographs have been especially commissioned for this publication.

Introduction

Paranormal in the Westcountry: two words that may puzzle some people.

What is the Paranormal? And where is the Westcountry?

Like a true Cornishman, I will try and answer the second question first.

Crispin Gill, writing an editorial in *The Western Morning News* in the newspaper's 125th year, asked 'Where is the West?' and then proceeded to reflect: 'But the Westcountry is not a precise term. It is not defined by Civil Service decree or constrained by county

'What is the Paranormal...'

'... and where is the Westcountry?'

4

boundaries. It is a mental thing, a reaction, a response to a stimulus. One might say it has all the exhilaration, all the infuriation, all the intoxication, of any normal love affair.'

That is a good definition because, at heart, the Westcountry defies neat classification. For the purpose of this book we have made it an area from Bristol to Land's End which conveniently happens to be Bossiney publishing territory.

Paranormal, according to the *Collins English Dictionary,* is defined in just three words: 'beyond normal explanation'.

But the word is bound to cause problems for any writer or publisher.

Brian Inglis in his excellent *The Paranormal, An Encyclopedia of Psychic Phenomena* opened with this warning: 'Anyone who attempts to describe paranormal phenomena is immediately confronted with a problem. For an influential minority of people, they do not exist. To relate accounts of them is consequently to court derision.'

Mr Inglis is right. But I suspect that 'influential minority' is smaller than we sometimes think. The subject is not upon its death bed. Moreover if we study history, we soon see that accounts of phenomena go deep back in time – to the early tribes – and that accounts have remained incredibly consistent. Ghosts and apparitions, witches and sorcerers have been with us through the ages.

It was back in 1974 that my first venture into this field was published: *Supernatural in Cornwall.* Then I had an open mind on Supernatural possibility, and hopefully I still have an open mind on most subjects.

Now, through a growing series of such titles and meetings related to those publications, I am quite convinced that there is a solid body of evidence relating to many aspects of the Paranormal field.

For example, I know that ghosts do exist.

The evidence is so overwhelming. I am more sure about the existence of ghosts than say the Duke of Wellington winning the

6

Battle of Waterloo or Hitler dying in that bunker in Berlin.

Admittedly, evidence and proof are difficult words in a Paranormal context – a wise judge might say in any context. Responsible intelligent people swear they have seen African witch doctors summon rain. In the last two decades researchers have produced some quite astonishing evidence which appears to strongly support traditional astrological beliefs.

I have not seen a ghost – but then can I be sure? I once had lunch with a young cricketer playing for Cornwall. At the time I didn't know he was going to batter his father and mother to death, put them in a wheel-barrow, and tip their bodies over a chunk of Cornish cliff.

One afternoon in November 1984 I was driving from Bodmin, back home to St Teath, when I saw a cyclist, some distance ahead coming in the opposite direction from Camelford. There was nothing vague or misty about him, and I wasn't day dreaming, but I

7

8

suddenly realized a little while on, we had not passed one another. The picture of him had been so vivid that I turned the car around. I drove for nearly a mile back down that road, but there was no sign of him or his cycle, and I am practically certain that, in the time scale, he could not have reached the next side turning.

Did I see a ghost? I don't know. I mention this to underline the fact that I am not overwriting anyone who appears inside the coming pages. My one and only certain experience has been described in detail in *Supernatural in Cornwall* and, in retrospect, thankfully it was a shared experience so there was no question of imagination or delusion.

Once you've had that kind of personal experience, once you start telling others about it, you find a Supernatural tennis match taking place. Your story encourages others to tell theirs. With so many experiences coming to the surface, you realize the man or woman, who has not had a strange experience, is rare – and possibly lacking in some kind of vision. I once interviewed a lady who owned a haunted house in Cornwall and, though she had heard inexplicable knockings on the doors of the house and had *seen* the same doors open and shut without the help of human hands, she still refused to believe the property haunted and dismissed *all* Supernatural possibility.

Personally I have interviewed a score or more people who have derived enormous benefit from spiritual healing, including Danny, a teenager from St Austell who was born with a hole in his heart. An operation was considered out of the question. 'Better to have a son fifty per cent alive than one hundred per cent dead' was how one doctor put it to his parents. Alan Nance, the well-known Cornish healer, started giving him healing, and within two months there was a transformation and before long Danny was a different boy, able to play football and cricket, ride a cycle and swim. That all happened more than a decade ago. I recently asked Alan Nance if Danny had survived. Alan smiled: 'He's fine. Emigrated to Canada; he's now a very active and successful man.'

In 1985 I was interviewed by Radio Cornwall, a programme to coincide with Hallowe'en, the most superstitious day in the calendar. In it interviewer Ted Gundry described me as someone 'who has got rather positive ideas on the Supernatural and things that go bump in the night'. I made no apology for that stance and went on to say: 'Having written five books of Supernatural content, and having interviewed over two hundred people I've come to the definite conclusion that Cornwall has probably more ghosts per acre than any other part of Britain.'

'Why do you think then that Cornwall has this affinity with the Supernatural?' probed the genial Ted.

'I'm not one hundred per cent sure, probably a combination of things... first, we're a Celtic county and I think we, Cornish, are more attuned to Supernatural and psychic matters than most other people. The remoteness of the region, the fact that you get a strong sense of the past here. You only have to go somewhere like the Hurlers, those standing stones on the edge of Bodmin Moor, and you feel quite close to the long ago – I think it was Sven Berlin, the sculptor, who said the division between past and present in Cornwall is very thin, and I know precisely what he means.'

Later in the same interview, we touched on the subject of evidence when Ted asked about favourite haunted areas, and I mentioned North Cornwall, with 'probably the most substantial evidence, and I use that word carefully, because I do consider that people have provided evidence. At St Nectan's Glen, for example, which is just off the road which links Boscastle and Tintagel... many people have claimed to have seen ghostly monk figures there and, of course, St Nectan had a shrine at that spot.'

Ted Gundry concluded our conversation by asking: 'Tell me,

**'... many areas in the Westcountry have a
particularly haunted and haunting
quality...'**

Michael, will you be keeping an eye open perhaps this All Souls
Eve, Hallowe'en Night?'

'Oh yes,' I replied, 'but I am keeping my eyes and ears open all
the year round because the fascinating thing about the Supernatural
is that ghosts appear anywhere and everywhere and not just in old
buildings. I've met people who have encountered them in modern
places. A few years ago I met a family who were driven out of a
council house by some very strange frightening happenings. So it's
not something that's either belonging to old buildings or one

11

Left: **'Dartmoor especially fires speculation.'**
Above: **'Exmoor, in a different way, fuels Supernatural possibility.'**

particular day. I think ghostly possibility surrounds us all the time, night and day throughout the calendar.'

Naturally on that occasion our thoughts were on Cornwall, but I equally believe many areas in the Westcountry have a particularly haunted and haunting quality – something the President of the Ghost Club will be discussing later.

Dartmoor especially fires speculation. The poet Ronald Duncan, crossing the moor, said he was reminded of a line from Tennyson, for here 'shadows of the world appear'. Exmoor, in a different way, fuels Supernatural possibility. I once rode across a large track of it, and can understand why both places have had so many hauntings.

13

Exmoor has none of Dartmoor's cruelty or desolation, but there is still mystery and magic to be found.

People, too, come into the reckoning in a very significant way. I can, for example, call in on my good friend Joan Bettinson who lives on Bodmin Moor and discuss all kinds of Paranormal subjects easily and naturally. Joan is a 'wise woman'. Some might call her a 'white witch'. She charms warts and ringworm. She can even do her healing over the telephone – as my wife Sonia will readily confirm. She also reads tea cups. Joan, in her quiet Cornish way, is quite a character. Once almost every village boasted its charmer, but now they are becoming a rare breed. I came to know Joan through Cornish bush telegraph – we, country people, still use that form of communication.

In the several years I was Acora's publisher and ghost writer, I saw time and again how his clairvoyancy confounded people – including myself. On one famous occasion before TV cameras in Bristol, he was asked about the future of the then local MP Tony Benn and, to my embarrassment, he proceeded to predict that, in the coming year, Benn would be trying to get into No. 10 Downing Street. On the journey home, I had the difficult business of explaining to him that this couldn't possibly happen as Harold Wilson, the then Prime Minister, would only go if he were beaten in a General Election. A few months later, I was lunching in West Cornwall, when someone burst into the room and announced the shock news: 'Harold Wilson is resigning as Prime Minister.' Within hours of that announcement Tony Benn was a candidate for Prime Minister.

The remarkable thing about this Romany soothsayer is that he had next to no schooling. He once confessed to me: 'I prefer to read palms to words in a book!' Another astonishing fact about Acora is he started making predictions at the age of seven. And his grandmother recognised he had the gift of second sight before that. 'They tell me I was about three or four,' he told me as we talked in his *vardo* (Romany for caravan), 'and the family were out in the country, somewhere in the wilds of Dartmoor. It was a hot summer's day and I wanted an ice-cream, but my father explained it was impossible in a place like that. "Go down the hill and turn right," I told him. Maybe just to keep me quiet, they went down the hill and turned right, and there, coming up the road, was an ice-cream van. Immediately my grandmother knew I had the gift.'

'Wise woman' Joan Bettinson: 'I came to know Joan through Cornish bush telegraph.'

Basically on this journey across the Westcountry, I have gone for the interview approach. I have had the luck to be given interviews by men and women, with particular gifts, and stories to tell. An old hand at interviewing and no new boy to the whole Paranormal field, I rate them all *people of integrity*. Of course, the best of us can be fooled or deluded, but I am quite convinced the vast majority of these accounts – and possibly all of them – are solidly true – as solidly so as say Rough Tor on Bodmin Moor, or St Michael's Church at Brentor or the Quantocks ranging across the lovely Somerset landscape.

Educated cynics baffle me more than 'psychic' crack-pots – and I have met a few of both varieties. The former give me greater concern because they should know better. But I am growing more tolerant, more understanding. I was puzzled and hurt, more than fifteen years ago, when a doctor – a lay preacher to boot – almost dismissed me as a lunatic when I asked his opinion on spiritual healing. I wondered how he coped with all that healing from the New Testament on Sunday mornings. Now I can't help wondering how he's coping with the Hereafter!

There has been a tremendous change in the climate in the Westcountry in the last ten to fifteen years. When I began researching and writing *Supernatural in Cornwall* more than one person thought I ought to be locked up and a very experienced author told me, 'I'm doubtful whether you'll sell that print run.' Not only has the book outlived that particular author, but it's gone into several reprints and is one of Bossiney's six top sellers.

Today the climate is very different, and I have a hunch it's because the world has grown in some ways – not all – into such a terrible place. I have a suspicion too the Church has somehow failed to get its message across – that's a dangerous generalization perhaps – but those empty pews rather reinforce the view. Consequently more and more people are turning to old ways.

Despite its brief definition in the dictionary, I have taken Paranormal to be a wide landscape. *I Ching*, tarot cards, healing, psychic painting, mediumship, ghosts and psycho-expansion are only some of the subjects featured. I make no apology for devoting a good measure of space and energy to ways and means of probing the future because down the ages Man has looked for some system to bring order to his life. He has wanted to 'see' his future, control his destiny and, above all, to multiply his fortune. The thousands of women and men, who read their horoscopes each morning, and the vast army of punters who back 'lucky numbers' rather than study 'form' are all living evidence of this centuries-old desire.

Some people may see these chapters as little more than an interesting collection of unusual beliefs and practices. Others will see them as vital, relevant contributions to Life itself.

All the subjects, to me, are just one – they all belong to the Paranormal.

I Ching – *Rosemary Clinch*

At this point on my Paranormal journey I attempted to go back in time – to China 3,000 years ago – and in a sense I did.

Rosemary Clinch, a fellow Bossiney author, who lives at Littleton-on-Severn, near Bristol, has been practising *I Ching* for a number of years. The *I Ching* is one of the oldest, most respected oracle books known to man, drawing its basic philosophy from ancient China, and Rosemary has found it immensely helpful in both her private and business lives.

A Cancer subject, Rosemary Clinch made her debut for Bossiney in 1984 when she contributed a chapter on 'Strange Sightings & Mystical Paths' in *Strange Somerset Stories:* on the subject of UFOs and ley lines. More recently, she has written *Supernatural in Somerset,* a fascinating exploration and series of interviews in Somerset.

One perceptive reviewer has likened her writing to that characteristic of the great James Cameron who told a string of editors: 'If you want the facts, you can get 'em from Reuters. I'll look *beyond* the facts for you.' David Foot in the Introduction to her *Unknown Bristol* reflected: 'I get the firm impression that Rosemary Clinch relishes looking round the corners and under the pavement stones...'

All these are qualities which make her ideal in the Occult field – the very word Occult means 'that which is secret' or 'that which is hidden'.

'First of all,' she said, 'it might be a good thing to explain as simply as possible the *I Ching* itself or the Oracle of Change as it is called. It is used by the people of the East in all kinds of professions, by philosophers, by businessmen and ordinary people... those who are seeking guidance for the future. That's really what the *I Ching* is: to speak with the Oracle, to obtain guidance for any future plans.

Rosemary Clinch: '... has written *Supernatural in Somerset,* **a fascinating exploration and series of interviews in Somerset.'**

Yang: Yin:

Hexagram		Month	Hexagram		Month
☰☷	5 20	**February**	☷☵	8 24	**August**
☰☳	7 22	**March**	☷☶	8 24	**September**
☰☱	6 21	**April**	☷☴	9 24	**October**
☰☰	6 22	**May**	☷☷	8 23	**November**
☷☰	7 22	**June**	☷☳	7 22	**December**
☶☰	8 24	**July**	☷☶	6 21	**January**

**The twelve ruling hexagrams for each
month of the year, showing the Yang and
Yin forces rising and falling. Each month is
divided into two fortnights to reflect the
seasonal changes, spring and autumn
equinox, summer and winter solstice.**

'At its most simple it is a collection of 64 hexagrams... that is six
lines... these six lines contain broken and unbroken lines. Each
hexagram is a complete reading accompanied by a set of
interpretations. In other words, when you have worked out which
hexagram you are to consult, you also have, with it, a set of
commentaries, as they are called, which are the *insight* to what the
lines *mean*.

'A hexagram is obtained by asking a question and dividing yarrow
stalks of a certain length and number. You can also use coins, but if
you wish to know the maximum then stalks are the best method.

'The lines are said to represent everything in life which is basic and their opposites: male and female, the yang, the male, and the yin, the female. Then there are sons and daughters, water and fire, all those things that are basic to us. They even represent all our basic attributes and feelings like love and hate. As well they represent the seasons. Each month has got its own hexagram which rules it. But the most important thing about the *I Ching* is it reflects all those things that do not stay the same. It says that we are always subjected to change and so within the wisdom of the *I Ching* lies the answers or the way in which we can fit in to all the changes that are in and around us.

'From a mathematical point of view the *I Ching* is based on the binary system and, of course, this is used today in computers. It is only when studying the lines that the complexity of their meaning becomes apparent.

'The Oracle contains a formidable amount of information. In fact, it is not unlike a computer. There is a great store of knowledge within its pages, but this can only be obtained *by practice.*

'It is said that the Oracle originated some 4,000 years ago during the Long Chan period and tradition says the lines were discovered on the back of an ancient tortoise. Some tortoises were considered heavenly in those days. Emperor Fu Hsi lived over 4,500 years ago and one day he noticed the patterns on the Heavens and the animals and even on his own body. These fascinated the Emperor to the extent he devised the eight basic patterns of lines which constituted the 64 readings. The eight basic patterns of lines are sets of three. In other words these sets of three interact in various ways and this is why the whole thing is very complicated.

'To go back further in history it is also said that the future was told in China by the burning of a shoulder blade from a cow while at the same time asking a question. They used to inscribe or write on the bone the question they wanted to ask. Then the position of the cracks in the bone produced by the heat would give the interpretation. Whatever its beginning the *I Ching* has always been regarded as important in the way one should live one's life.

'As far as recognition of the *I Ching* in the western world is concerned, it actually happened comparatively recently. About a hundred years ago it became known to the western world, but people were inclined to look upon it as a bit of a curiosity. It was around the 1930s that the psychologist Dr Jung made known his

findings: a German, Richard Wilkelm, wrote an interpretation of the *I Ching* and Dr Jung wrote the forward.'

Peter Underwood in his scholarly *Dictionary of the Occult & the Supernatural* has written: 'The remarkable aptness and helpfulness obtained from the serious use of *I Ching* has been repeatedly remarked upon by those who persevere with the system, and it seems likely that the act of asking questions and interpreting the replies prepares the mind to enter a state similar to that reached in accepted forms of meditation. The great psychologist C. G. Jung believed that the symbols and words in *I Ching* conveyed messages directly to the unconscious mind.'

In conversation, Rosemary Clinch is an ideal interviewee, her words coming easily, naturally. Someone, who recently interviewed her on radio, called her a 'natural communicator'. Outside and beyond all that, she has the gift of putting herself in the other person's shoes.

At this point she recalled her genesis in this field: 'When I first read the *I Ching* during my studies of the Supernatural I found it reinforced my belief in my own natural intuition which is something strong in me. Since then I have become more and more convinced that its use can help to expand awareness which we all lack in the hidden realms of the mind. I believe that in the mind lies the key to many things and with the *I Ching* I exercise my mind. It has been a positive guidance to me in my work and in my personal life on many occasions. The best results have come from several days or weeks of working on a particular problem and this is the beauty of the *I Ching*: you start by asking it a question and invariably it will give you a reason for asking another question. So as you move on: asking one question and getting an answer, you can build up a very detailed picture of what is waiting for you there in the future.

'You have to be very careful when consulting the Oracle. You consider the question very carefully indeed. It has to be simple. It has to be precise and direct. You have to make absolutely sure that you don't get carried away and want too much all at once. In life, as you probably know, there is always more than one alternative so there will invariably be more than one question to be asked.

Left: **Dr C. G. Jung 'would sit for hours under a hundred-year-old pear tree referring to the Oracle...'**

'You take travel, for example. If I have no alternative but to travel on a Monday, say next Monday, then obviously I am thinking about Monday. And I would choose to say "Is next Monday a good day for travel?" I'd say the day, which Monday, and the fact that I want to know if it is a good day, so the hexagram that I finally arrive at would give me an idea of whether there will be any pitfalls. If I'm lucky the one question will be enough, but supposing it mentions something evil, I won't really know what this evil is. The next question, though, would not be "What is the evil?", because there will be a lot of evil occuring on that Monday, not necessarily to me. You have to be very, very specific, so the next question would be "What is the evil I will meet next Monday?"

'The Oracle can be very precise, provided *you* are precise. The wisdom of *I Ching* lies in your ability to tune in to the interpretations of the lines. You have to acquire a feeling for the text. You have to let it flow through the mind. You are literally reading between the lines and understanding what the Oracle is trying to say *to you*, for it's to the deep levels of the mind that the Oracle speaks – and here we come to intuition again. It's here that the intuition lies. Speaking with the Oracle you develop your intuition.'

To the true disciples of *I Ching*, the world is not made up of particles – of time and space – but everything is part of everything else. Reality, then, is essentially change. The stream one paddled in yesterday is not the river one swims in today. The Universe is seen as a moving pattern.

The *I Ching* does not regard the past, the present and the future as fixed. It treats time and fate as dynamic and *flowing* – and Rosemary Clinch conveys this philosophy thoughtfully, perceptively in her book *Supernatural in Somerset*.

'Somerset as much as any county has its share of the Supernatural, ghosts, poltergeists and people who have had strange experiences or gifts which are part of the Paranormal... Somerset has always had some special kind of magic for me,' she has written.

Atmosphere, healing, dowsing, fork-bending and strange encounters are only some of the subjects featured inside her pages. Characters like astrologer Roger Elliot, healers Barney Camfield and Tim Tiley, mystics Mary and John Drinkwater, fork-bender Heloise Gravenor, and Austin Wookey, philosopher of the

24

Rosemary Clinch practising *I Ching* **at home.**

Somerset countryside, are among those interviewed – there is even an encounter with a lady who believes she was King Arthur in an earlier life.

Moreover, Rosemary Clinch personifies the *I Ching* approach in her day-to-day living. When earlier we collaborated on *Unknown Somerset,* I wrote: 'Reading her pages – for me – has been a fascinating experience: the way she has justified the inclusion of a well-known city like Bath, her talent for going down into the cellar and finding the *real* story, or her recent experience in Taunton, something that defied all human explanation. These are only two examples of how she makes us turn the pages eagerly.

'Thanks to Rosemary, I now find myself travelling across the county with a deeper insight and understanding, a sharper sense of

**'Somerset has always had a special kind of
magic for me.'**

anticipation. Her wanderings conceal real art, careful planning and
intuition.'

Hereabouts, Rosemary recalled a major family decision.

'My son Craig is a very personal part of my life and before he
went into the RAF he said: "Oh, come on, mum, tell me what the
I Ching says about my going into the RAF."

'It was a very difficult reading, and the answers we got said
virtually what has happened, but at the time I couldn't see it. What
it was saying to me through the lines, between the lines, was a
feeling that perhaps he couldn't cope with it all... not the
responsibilities or the work... but coping with being bored and this
is basically what has happened.'

26

Our discussion moved on to another area. 'It is very interesting, when you consider that I need to ask questions when consulting the Oracle. This also applies when I am dowsing, I need to ask a question. If I am looking for water I ask "Where is it?" When I am holding the dowsing rod, I have to have *the picture* of what I am seeking. Once again it is all in the mind. It's all in the inner self. The tieing in of one's inner self to some kind of force, that's around you, acts as a conductor. It is all very mysterious I agree, but over a period of years I have come to see it as a perfectly natural thing.

'Sometimes the Oracle captures my mind and I lose all awareness of what is going on around me. The Oracle is one book I am always prepared to get lost in.

'It's very good for the inner psyche to relax and the Oracle does help me to relax. After dividing the stalks, I am usually feeling very relaxed and happy.

'Confucius said: "If some years were added to my life I would give fifty to the study of the Oracle and might then escape falling into great error." That was in, I think, 481 BC when he was over seventy years old! And Dr Jung would sit for hours under a hundred-year-old pear tree referring to the Oracle. Rather like these two, I feel I could spend hours and hours...'

Ghost Hunter in the West –
Peter Underwood

The man, who has been called Britain's Ghost Hunter Supreme, is a regular visitor to the Westcountry.

He holidays annually in Cornwall, and ghostly trails have led him all over the South West.

For more than forty years Peter Underwood has probed the Supernatural. He has spent many hours of daylight and darkness in dozens of haunted houses, but he is not just a very distinguished ghost hunter, his interests are wide. A long-standing member of The Society for Psychical Research, Vice-President of the Unitarian Society for Psychical Studies, a member of The Folklore Society, The Dracula Society, and a former member of the Research Committee of the Psychic Research Organisation, he took part in the first official investigation into a haunting.

Peter Underwood has sat with mediums and conducted investigations at séances, been present at exorcisms, experiments at dowsing, precognition, clairvoyance, hypnotism and regression. He has also conducted world-wide tests in telepathy and extra-sensory perception. He possesses comprehensive files of alleged hauntings in every part of the British Isles and many countries overseas. His knowledge and experience have all resulted in his being consulted on psychic matters by the BBC and ITV.

President for a quarter of a century of the most respected and influential organization in this eerie field – The Ghost Club, which was founded back in 1862 'where mediums and materialists, spiritualists and sceptics meet on neutral ground' as the *New York*

Right: **Peter Underwood: 'Britain's Ghost Hunter Supreme' and President of the Ghost Club for more than a quarter of a century.**

Times once put it – Peter Underwood has almost certainly heard more first-hand ghost stories than any man alive or dead.

He has been described by objective observers as 'a veteran psychical researcher, representing the middle ground between scepticism and uncritical belief.' He has lectured, written and broadcast extensively.

'A good writer who knows his subject' was how Colin Wilson described him on BBC television. 'A walk with Mr Underwood can be a very nervy affair indeed,' reflected a reviewer for the *Yorkshire Evening Post.* 'The undisputed king of ghost hunters' said another critic.

The man himself believes the great majority of reported hauntings have 'a natural and mundane explanation'. But he is intensely interested in the minority – the other cases.

'Many cases of so-called hauntings,' he once said, 'can be explained without resorting to the Supernatural... Some can be attributed to psychosomatic disorders or disturbed personalities, hallucinatory effects or emotional difficulties. But there are also cases of hauntings that are reported by happy healthy people... where strange happenings transcend all known laws.

'Where this happens, and it *does* happen, the phenomenon reported is often identical to that reported from every part of the world and in every civilization since the beginning of recorded history.'

In his excellent book *The Ghost Hunters, Who They Are and What They Do,* he has written: '...I have had experiences that convince me that some "thing" or some force does exist about which we know little and over which we have no control. The work of the dedicated ghost hunter is to explore that realm of uncertainty with an open mind and carefully to preserve and record all his findings, and then one day, perhaps, we shall learn exactly what circumstances, what climatic conditions, what mental approach and what scientific instruments can prove to anyone that the study and examination of these subjects are important and far-reaching for all mankind.'

Here in the Westcountry Peter Underwood is the author of two bestsellers, *Ghosts of Devon* and *Ghosts of Cornwall,* and, more recently, *Ghosts of Somerset,* all published by Bossiney. Currently he is working on *Westcountry Hauntings.*

Having this strong Westcountry background as both ghost hunter and author, I asked him about the region. 'Whenever I am asked

'... the haunted ruins of Berry Pomeroy in Devon.'

which is the most haunted part of Britain,' he said, 'I have no hesitation in indicating the three adjoining counties of Cornwall, Devon and Somerset; that south-west corner of these islands which is almost a separate country with its own countryside, buildings and ideas, its individual inhabitants and its fascinating ghosts.

'I don't know why this should be so, although it is a fact that other isolated and "primitive" and "un-civilised" places are also very haunted: parts of East Anglia, Northern England and Scotland in particular, but then we have London, surely the most haunted place on earth with hardly a street that does not have a reported ghost!

'After almost half-a-century of serious interest in the whole realm of the paranormal but in spontaneous phenomena in particular –

ghosts and haunted houses – I remember with nostalgic happiness the days and the nights spent in pursuit of ghosts in the West of England and I look forward, with anticipative delight, to future expeditions to haunted places, for one day a haunting is going to make history by being scientifically authenticated – and I have a strong feeling that that momentous event is going to take place in Cornwall, or Devon or, possibly, Somerset. The undisputed documentative quality of testimony and variety of phenomena that have been reported from these three counties is quite remarkable.'

I asked him about favourite haunted sites here in the South West. 'It is over twenty years now since my wife and I first visited the haunted ruins of Berry Pomeroy in Devon,' he recalled. 'Over the intervening years we have been there in all seasons and at all times of the day and night and it never ceases to exude its individual atmosphere and magic. Here the physician to the Prince Regent saw the resident ghost whose appearance heralded the death of someone in the family, and so it proved on that occasion.

The Black House at Higher Brixham: '... has lingered in my memory long after.'

'The best-known story from Berry Pomeroy tells of two sisters who fell in love with the same man and one succeeded in luring her sister into the dungeon where she starved to death: her ghost, known as the Lady Margaret, is said to be seen to this day from time to time on the steps leading to the ruined dungeon, seeking to lure others to destruction.

'When a party of Ghost Club members visited Berry Pomeroy in 1983 we met two people who claimed to have experienced a strange impulse to proceed towards the ruined and dangerous dungeon – and they had no knowledge of the legend until we informed them. More recently I've received first-hand evidence of a similar nature from a visitor who wrote to me after reading one of my books in which I related the stories of ghosts at Berry Pomeroy. They, too, had not heard anything about the place being haunted when they went there. Within the last few months there have been reports of paranormal activity in the vicinity of these isolated ruins perched on a spur of the hillside, a place that seems to have been haunted for several hundred years; a place that has a strange and puzzling history; and a place with an atmosphere all its own and sometimes very frightening.

'Another haunted Devon property that has lingered in my memory long after I left it is the Black House at Higher Brixham. This case was brought to my attention by a friend some fifteen years ago and when the then owner showed me round and related the several ghostly associations, both my wife and I found ourselves affected by the ominous influence of the house. We were told of various incidents that could have had a natural explanation but more interestingly we learned, and subsequently verified, various incidents, auditory and visual in nature, that had been experienced by disinterested witnesses, including a police officer.

'The ghost figure of a monk and a squire reputedly haunt the Black House and one sound that has, or had, repeatedly been heard here was evidentially a paranormal recording of some kind, for the clatter of horses' hooves, sounding on cobble-stones, had echoed through the house, but the place where the sounds appeared to originate was a lawn, although nine feet below the lawn traces had been found of a cobbled yard that once belonged to a previous building.'

In his *Ghosts of Cornwall* Peter Underwood opened by saying: 'Cornwall is a land of mystery where, even today, in some hamlets and away from the busy roads, there is an atmosphere not altogether of this world. Once over the strangely winding Tamar and into Cornwall the visitor enters a mystic land and it is indisputable that visits to this Celtic County leave an indelible impression on the mind. Those who are lucky enough to return again and again never really escape from the enchantment of the place – or want to.

'Cornwall is full of ghosts. There are strange stories of diminutive figures, of silent and brooding forms, of invisible influences, of repeated appearances, of haunted houses and ghostly cities; it is a rich hunting ground for the ghost seeker and for those who appreciate the odd, the miraculous and the inexplicable. The ghosts of Cornwall are a varied bunch indeed.'

Naturally, our conversation now crossed the Tamar. 'Dockacre House at Launceston in Cornwall I first heard about when the occupant wrote to me following one of my broadcasts and I subsequently visited this fascinating house in the company of my friend James Turner, the poet and writer who loved Cornwall,' he recalled. 'The alleged haunting here has several interesting twists: the ghost of Nicholas Herle haunts the main hall – although he died in Hampstead; the sound of a flute being played is heard when a death is about to occur in the house – but a curious flute-stick that is preserved in the house – the only flute there – has been blocked at the ends and is incapable of being played by normal means; and a large and persistent bloodstain on the stairs marked the scene of a reputed murder – but it disappeared when the staircase treads were renewed.

'Dockacre House, built into the side of a hill and possessing several secret passages has a history of mysterious rappings, unexplained nocturnal opening and closing of doors, and pictures falling off the walls. I saw no ghost at Dockacre and only sensed a peaceful atmosphere but the mellow house, brooding and strangely quiet, seemed to exude a feeling of mysterious expectancy as though something very odd might happen here at any moment, as it certainly has in the past.'

From Cornwall our thoughts moved on to Somerset, an area which had fired Peter Underwood to write in *Ghosts of Somerset*: '... throughout its million acres are scores of romantic and historic

Right: **'Cornwall is full of ghosts...'**

houses, towns, villages and landscapes, many of them individual ghostly associations, many of them reputed to be haunted by singular paranormal activity and not a few have been the scene of repeated spectral appearances that totally defy rational explanation. Somerset is indeed rich hunting ground for the ghost enthusiast.'

At this point in our conversation, I asked him about the haunted quality of this county of cider, cheese and cricket.

'Somerset is full of mystery and magic,' he said. 'Much of the centre of the county still seems remote from the bustle and hurry of the present day; resting almost, waiting to be discovered, with its little villages linked by roads that are little more than tracks for farmers and their cattle. Nestling among these lanes are several houses with ghosts a-plenty.

'Take for example Gaulden Manor with its ghostly grey lady, phantom cavaliers and the shade of a monk in the Turberville Bedroom and another in the Bishops' Garden. Once the famous phantom coach of the Turbervilles visited this lovely house but since the disappearance of the Turberville family, the coach has disappeared too. Here, where a ghost apparently manifested in daylight when I was there in 1984, there is, it seems, a ghostly little black and white dog in the garden, a recent acquisition, or so I was told in 1985. There is a strange little story concerning this phantom animal. Some months previously one of the owners of Gaulden Manor had buried a black and white chihuahua by request in the garden, to be near his father whose statue can be seen in the garden. A little girl of about ten years old, visiting the house, said, "I have just seen a little black and white dog go into the hedge." She pointed to a tan-coloured chihuahua and said: "A dog like that." No dogs are allowed in the house or garden and the little girl was asked whether it could have been a rabbit. "No," she replied, quite definitely. "It was a little dog like yours but he was black and white."

'And what are we to make of Glastonbury? Did Joseph of Arimathea bring with him in AD 60 the cup of the Last Supper and is it buried in what is called to this day Chalice Hill? Was a sprig from the Crown of Thorns the first Christmas Rose? Certainly experts from Kew and elsewhere are puzzled and say it is the only

Left: **'Somerset... mystery and magic.'**

'And what are we to make of Glastonbury?'

thorn in England to blossom at Christmas. The White Thorn of Glastonbury is strangely awesome and so is the dungeon where the last Abbot spent his final night in 1524; even the practical guides admit that the area of the dungeon window, still barred and close to the ground, retains something of the horror it once knew.

'As I recount these stories, memories flood in of happy times in the Westcountry and oddly strange and puzzling incidents. There was the night we spent on Dartmoor when our dog, quiet and unperturbed in all weather and veteran of many a visit to a haunted house, simply would not settle but continually wandered round and round, growling, and so on all night through... there was the visit to a haunted ruin when the whole place seemed to shimmer and fade and change completely for a second... there was the chilling sensation on a hot summer day at Chambercombe Manor years ago when I learned that I was standing on the spot where the ghost invariably materialized – and I couldn't move hand or foot! There was the time when a ghost was seen standing by my side in a haunted manor in Somerset... and the cottage haunted by a murderer where phantom raps answered those that I had speculatively made...

'The sympathetic enquirer into the mysteries and the legends and the ghost stories of the Westcountry will find himself following many strange trails, discovering many secrets of the past yet to be unearthed, and perhaps catch a glimpse of a form or being that was once as we are now. And I envy him every inch of his journey!'

Psychic All-Rounder – *Shirley Wallis*

Shirley Wallis *is* a psychic all-rounder.

She may be best known to the Plymouth public through her stars column, each week, in *The Plymouth Star,* but she is also a healer, practises psycho-expansion *and* reads tarot cards. She is extremely well read in the whole varied psychic world. Ask her about, say, knowledge by numbers or symbols in the sky, and she will invariably come up with some thoughtful comment – or probing question.

A Devonian, an Aquarian subject with brown eyes, she lives at Plymstock on the edge of Plymouth.

Talking with Shirley Wallis you get the impression she is equally at home in the here and now or the long ago – or probing the future. I have never asked her, but I have a hunch she doesn't worry too much about dividing lines or labels. More than once I have interviewed her in psycho-expansion sessions, and it is you – the interviewer – who have to remind yourself that you're here, firmly rooted in this thing we call the present. She has, it seems, the ability to take you with her to another time and place – but more of that later.

In addition to her work in the various Supernatural areas, she runs the family home, does a full time job, often involving long hours, and is an example for all those people who complain 'I haven't got the time!' She quite simply packs an enormous amount into her day or week.

She talks well. I have had long conversations with her, listened to her on radio, have even joined her in a broadcast. She is a skilful

Right: **Shirley Wallis – 'a psychic all-rounder'.**

communicator, and I have a feeling, one day, she will write a very worthwhile book.

At the beginning of our conversation, I asked about astrology.

'A person's individual chart,' she explained, 'is a map – to me – of their potential energies. It's their force field, and astrology enables me to understand through this unique map how they can use their different energies, as described by the placing of the planets.

'I have just become a grandmother and was present at the birth, and so was able to get the exact time of my granddaughter's entry into the world... her chart is going to be a source of great delight because of the potential I can already see there.

'So forewarned is forearmed. In relationships, where we want to explore compatability between couples, both charts can be investigated and placed together to see where areas of stress may occur. Or if you want to choose a good time for a business venture or any important project, astrology is the tool which provides the signposts.

'In terms of a person's horoscope, astrology is a diagnostic tool, which has been given to man, to understand his roots and infinity and the higher laws of creation which govern him. It's not an end unto itself, it's just the beginning...

'So if we have a look at planets in our solar system and what type of energy they describe, remember they are symbolic. So with Mercury, the placing shows how we think and express ourselves. With Venus, well-known planet of love, how we relate to others. With Mars, it's how we use up energy and talents to get really what we want. Jupiter shows how we enjoy ourselves and expand our understanding, while with Saturn what self-discipline and strength of character we have, and this will be tested in the areas in which it falls in the chart. Uranus, the ways in which we are inventive and creative and original and unusual, the same word really. Neptune is how we can best help others. It's our spiritual mode, it's best described also as how we can use others in a way. Pluto is how we can grow, through deepening our self-knowledge, and the Sun, our sun sign, shows our deepest goals in life and what we really want, and the Moon is showing how we feel and respond emotionally. So all of those descriptions are of energy or vibrations which have been measured mathematically, because it's been found that the planets actually pulsate at certain rates, making magnetic fields... reflecting and describing how man thinks and feels.

Zodiac signs: Aries, Taurus, Gemini and Cancer...

43

Leo, Virgo, Libra and Scorpio...

Sagittarius, Capricorn, Aquarius and Pisces.

There is a mental body, a spiritual body and an astral body, which is a feeling, emotional body, all of these make up man. These are the non-physical expression of man in the world and they work in a magnetic way. So all these bodies are linked by flows of energy, magnetic in nature, and we can see this flow sometimes in a person's aura and the colours predominating in that aura. So cosmically speaking, the aura of planets in our solar system is based upon the same colour symbolism as that of the human aura. Consequently everyone has certain qualities outlined by astrology.'

Our discussion now moved on to psycho-expansion. Exponents of psycho-expansion claim to have the ability to go back or forward in time.

Readers of *Mysteries in the Devon Landscape* will know of Shirley Wallis's ability to travel back in time, to recall vividly, with remarkable clarity and attention to detail.

Her time travel visit to Wistman's Wood on Dartmoor produced some diamond-sharp descriptions. Here she found a seam of quartz running through the centre underground, and she came away from this strange wood refreshed and full of energy.

I have twice interviewed Shirley when she has regressed. On both occasions she seemed to sink into a trance – the impression was one of self-hypnosis – and in this state her tone of voice became lower in key. Interestingly, though, there was no plateau of emotion. At times she appeared amused, but on other parts of her time travel she was genuinely troubled.

I now asked her how she began with psycho-expansion – and how she defined it.

'In 1979 I started classes in psycho-expansion in Plymouth, with Barney Camfield. An opportunity arose through a broadcast and a television programme and I started that way. Of course previously I'd been interested in the possibilities of reincarnation, and this just gave me the opportunity to further that. Psycho-expansion allows people to explore and develop their sense of awareness, and it's a technique which eventually allows the mind to move in time and space through understanding the self.

Right: **'Her time travel visit to Wistman's Wood on Dartmoor produced some diamond-sharp descriptions.'**

'The technique is relaxing, it relieves stress, making for a much happier balanced mind and body. Through psycho-expansion, I did have some extraordinary experiences of former lives, but basically it's the experience that counts much more than the possibility of the whole recall being correct and true. Now, the more you do psycho-expansion and link the pieces of information together, the more you realise there is an on-going story which is here, now, operating in this particular physical body. It is through the experiences that you have in psycho-expansion that you develop your sense of awareness and your psyche. Hence the title psycho-expansion. It's expanding the psyche and if it does nothing else for some people it teaches them how to be still for a little while and relax. In itself that has a healing quality of its own. My ability to move in time and space allows me to research and investigate historical dates sometimes, and sites of archaeological interest, but it does take practice. This is where astrology is complementary to psycho-expansion because it has developed my understanding of cosmic energy.

'I was coming up with so much symbolism in psycho-expansion and found myself operating with astrological symbolism that I *knew* that I really had to go into astrology. Well, that was my road. It was quite obvious and that's what I did. I know I'm back to astrology, but you see, for me, the two things link in very definitely. I find, since I'm also a healer, these two techniques are very helpful in uncovering the cause of disease that really is a dis-ease in a person's mind and body.

'So psycho-expansion is a technique. Anybody can learn the technique, but everyone is operating on their own level and according to that level; it doesn't matter what the level is, they will develop their psyche. I found that it's like energy flow, energy never stops flowing or moving but it does reach peaks and troughs, and so it is with life, you might hear somebody say they're going through a certain phase. Well, that's what I mean really. One has phases of peak alps with exploring things, one has a phase with one particular type of exploration.'

In an earlier interview, when Shirley had regressed, she came out of that seemingly trance-like state gradually, like someone awakening, giving the impression she had travelled a long way, more than the suggestion of a tired traveller coming to a destination – or returning home.

'Do these journeys in time tire you?'

'Physically they don't tire me. It makes me very mentally in tune with what's going on around me. I don't very often want to leave... it's quite uncanny sometimes how you can come back with extraordinary information about which you know nothing in this life. But when you're *in there* you know every blooming detail, and I suspect that all of the discoveries that have been made have been done... not suspect, I know that they've been done on those levels, plucking out of the whole the discovery. Any new discovery, you see, because really the whole cosmic scene is a giant's computer and, if your intent is right, you are going to get onto the level where you get the right information.'

Now our discussion turned to healing, and here I had better say I have received healing from Shirley Wallis: a simple laying-on of hands on the spine, no ritual, no praying. Yet almost immediately I felt a heat and warmth and a sense of wellbeing sustained for something like 72 hours.

So I asked her how healing works.

'It works,' she said, 'but it's so difficult to explain. With healing two things come together. The magnetic force fields show that we can, by intent, if you like, wring out, in us, the content of our healing flow of energy. It's really as simple as that. It's quite natural: here you are, a whole bundle of force field energy giving loving concern for another's problem which has sort of gone up the spout for the moment. It's out of tune. You can really call it a force field between the two of you: the healer and the patient, and it just seems to work. That's really not good enough in scientific terms but it has been shown that if you link yourself up to an electro-encephalograph, you can measure those energies between healer and patient. You have to use some intelligence with healing and use it in a very intelligent manner by becoming a channel through which the cosmic energies can flow through the healer to the patient, and all the ways of applying healing, through the feet, through the pressure points of the body, through acupunture, it's *all* saying exactly the same thing.

'Nothing is different. It's just a different technique of using the flow. I think one of the problems has been: "Which technique shall we use? They're all so confusing. I'll try this and I'll try that." The fact remains that everybody's level is different, and one technique may suit better than another, may be much more beneficial... your force field would reveal whether you're in tune with your healer or with the person with whom you're having a dialogue. It's very difficult not to bring up astrological terms all the time in one's daily life... we, who use astrology, don't do it to confound everyone else. It's just like shorthand; an astrological term can often be worth a couple of pages of conventional description.

'Even in healing I find myself coming back to astrology because – to me – it will often uncover a whole problem area... what's caused the patient the distress, this *dis-ease.*'

Our discussion moved on to tarot cards – a subject which has puzzled me since an experience in January 1974. A clairvoyant visited us at Bossiney. A sensitive character, a potter and painter, Pip loved delving into the magical and the mystical. Her partner had died the year before, but she assured me she had seen him recently.

'Michael,' she said, looking up from the tarot cards on the table, 'you're going to write a book about the Supernatural and it's related to Cornwall.'

I had no reason to suppose she knew anything about my researches into the subject or that I had masses of notes lying in the bottom drawer of my desk.

Incredibly within a fortnight I was looking at a small wooden box in Tintagel Church containing her ashes. She had died in her sleep on the date of her late partner's birthday. 'It's not a sad occasion,' said Sonia as we made our way out of the churchyard. 'Pip was always half in this world and half in the next.'

By the end of the month, I started writing, turning those notes in the bottom drawer into a book. *Supernatural in Cornwall* was the result, one of the titles which helped to establish Bossiney Books.

Now I had the chance to ask Shirley Wallis a question which had been buzzing around in my mind for more than a decade.

'How can a thing like tarot cards really help to map out a person's future. Isn't the fall of the cards all luck and chance?'

'I have got to know the cards,' she explained. 'Though I'm no expert, I've devised a scheme: the lay of the cards describes the horoscope. Again, what we're doing is using a tool, just like astrology, just like pyscho-expansion – but I am of the mind that nothing is all luck or chance.

'Tarot cards are an immediate expression of the energies at play *today*. Throw them again tomorrow and you will find possibly a whole different scene. Some of the things would link, but you have

**'How can a thing like tarot cards really help
to map out a person's future?'**

the day's happenings as it were. You have the whole answer in your
own hands but you need some signposts, you need guidelines in
order to make some sort of judgment and this is *why* I use the
tarot.

'I don't say: "OK. What sort of man are you going to meet?" I
don't go into any prediction area on that sort of level, but what I do
know is what the person, in front of me, is not telling, because there
is often a lot of hidden stuff. While it is delving in a sense, if we are
to get anywhere and apply a loving kindness to the situation, one
really needs to know, or intuitively know, *where* the real
psychological trouble lies.

'Yes, the tarot is rather like traffic lights, giving clear-cut signs.
The tarot system helps me with direct questions and because it's

51

quick to answer, I value it, it gives me something to work on. It's also a focal point to have someone there. To have them take part in the discovery and to see the picture really unfold before them.'

Shirley now led on to Karma, that belief whereby every act – in this life – receives either punishment or reward.

'Man is the creator of Karma every moment,' she said, 'and it is very important for a person to learn the *meaning of the moment* because an individual could spend his entire life searching for what he was in former incarnations. He may be fortunate enough to find out or he may delude himself... we're not getting in touch with the real meaning of life unless we realize that this ability to locate ourselves in the here and now is where our greatest functioning capacity develops because it's through *this* development that our evolution really unfolds... it's extremely easy to blame one's failures on past life.

'So Karma exists. It's very real but it's not beyond man's means to deal with it and overcome. Past and future have less to do with man's ability to function. Naturally past and future have a strong influence over how an individual perceives the now. They both exist but we should neither linger in what we've done or failed to do. Nor should we worry about what we have to do. We should simply act and do – and become. Then we've got no time to analyse our actions because that means going back to the past again, and we've no time to feel insecure because that means worrying about the future. Instead we've got all the time in the world to live this present moment of reality.

'Psycho-expansion experience shows that we are responsible for every action and thought we have from the very beginning. It's what Yoga and meditation and any discipline is saying. It's a lifetime's work, many lifetimes in fact, and it's very necessary for us to go through all those experiences because that is what we chose to do with our free will.

'Look at a football match and see the emotional response from the crowd and all the energy at play – tremendous response there, but it can get out of hand. If that energy had direction, it could be put to enormous good because the same energy is creative. It could bring so many harmonious things into more positive play, instead of destructive play.

'We come right down to the very smallest living creature having its own force field. So cause and effect are essential learning.'

Shirley Wallis and I ended in a way where we had begun: with astrology or, more specifically, with her weekly stars column.

'When I started in astrology, I could see how awfully mundane it could be if you were to generalize in a solar way in a newspaper, day to day or week to week, but I thought it was a challenge to be offered this possibility. I thought it wasn't really going to be very satisfying, but it has turned out to be extraordinary... each week a little story unfolds for each of the signs and after a year of developing the skill, I'm finding it absolutely fascinating.

'I'm really never putting down anything on paper which doesn't give *some* hope. It might be a ghastly day in general aspect, but you will get a gift from whatever you're going to learn and put to use later on. From my point of view my weekly horoscope column is very seriously dealt with, but it should be fascinating fun and enjoyed every step of the way, demonstrating that there is always light at the end of the tunnel.'

The Significance of Numbers

It was while working with Romany clairvoyant Acora that I first began to understand the significance of numbers in the Occult world.

That may not be strictly true, though, because, even as a boy, for some reason I cannot recall, 47 was my lucky number and curiously the only match-winning innings I ever played at cricket was in a game at Bristol, where on a perfect wicket I had the luck to score 47 not out.

Looking back I realise 4 and 7 independently are numbers which have often worked well for me.

Moreover, I have never been worried about 13, which many people regard as a very unlucky number, so I was interested to learn from Acora's wife Jeannette, another traveller, that she had no fears about 13.

'Superstition is a very personal thing,' she told me, 'in that we make our own. If I'm having a flutter, I'll often go for number 7 or 13. Personally, I've never found Friday the 13th especially unlucky. I have known a lot of good things to happen on Friday 13th.'

Through contact with both Acora and Jeannette, I have come to put a lot of faith in the old Romany saying: 'Think lucky and you'll be lucky.' I don't think it's merely wishful thinking. Highly intelligent students of human behaviour have come to the conclusion that if we *feel* lucky, the odds are we'll attract good luck.

Nevertheless, numbers have fascinated people through the centuries. Ever since Pythagoras stated: 'The world is built upon the power of numbers,' men and women of all colours and creeds

Left: **Madam Jeannette: 'Superstition is a very personal thing in that we make our own.'**

have tried to fathom their secrets. The ancient Egyptians attached considerable significance to numbers and used them as a means of predicting the future. The movements of the planets, one season following another – they're all governed by the laws of mathematics or, more simply, numbers.

Back in 1980 Jeannette and I collaborated: a chapter on numbers for Acora's annual publication. We did some digging and here were some of our findings.

1 is a masculine number – it's believed the male was created first. This is the Leo number. It stands for action and achievement.

2 is for justice and equality, maintaining that there are two sides to every question. This is the female number and aids Gemini.

3 was considered the perfect number by ancient philosophers. It's lucky for Pisces. The old Pagan religions are peppered with the number 3 – the Priestesses sitting upon the 'tripod of truth'.

4 represents the four elements: fire, air, earth and water. Aquarius and Virgo are both helped by this number. Sometimes a mixture of 4 and 3 can produce very exciting results.

5 preaches five duties: prayer, fasting, purification, alms and the pilgrimage to Mecca. This is the soul number and does well for Cancer and Capricorn. David chose five stones with which to slay Goliath.

6 was used by the Jews who considered it a sacred number – the world was created in six days and primitive people believed the double triangle was a charm strong enough to ward off evil spirits. Libra and Sagittarius will benefit from it.

7 is the most mysterious number of all, due to the seven planets. To the Romans and the Greeks it was a symbol of good fortune and will prove lucky for Aries folk.

8 was a lucky number in old Egypt because eight people went in each boat on processions along the Nile. Mathematically it's double the strength of strong number 4 – and is favoured by all Taurus subjects.

9 was a feared number because the monster Hydra had 'nine heads', and the Fallen Angels in *Paradise Lost* fell nine times. 9 is also a healing number and works well for Scorpio.

These were only just some of our findings. It is, in fact, a vast fascinating subject – almost as old as history itself. Since that initiation, I have gone on quietly studying, digesting facts and figures in this field.

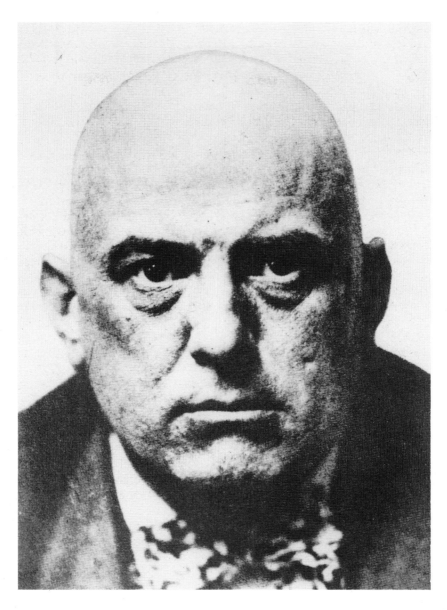

Aleister Crowley '... pure mathematics is our link with the rest of the universe...'

The serious student of numerology is firmly convinced each name we bear is no accident – no whim or fancy of parents – but a code to which the expert sensitive numerologist holds the key.

Here is how an American, Florence Campbell, explained the process: 'The Soul has taken many journeys in the past and knows its present needs. The Soul wants progress upwards on the Great Spiral and chooses for the incarnating ego the vowels whose total shall accomplish this purpose... There is a long "Dark Cycle" before the child is born, and during this Dark Cycle the vibrations that are to label the new life are so impressed upon the subconscious minds of the parents that they are compelled to carry out the plan.'

Aleister Crowley had this to say: 'We know infinitesimally little of the material universe. Our detailed knowledge is so contemptibly minute, that it is hardly worth reference, save that our shame may spur us to increased endeavour. Such knowledge as we have got is of a very general and abstruse, of a philosophical and almost magical character. This consists principally of the conceptions of pure mathematics. It is, therefore, almost legitimate to say that pure mathematics is our link with the rest of the universe and with "God".'

There are, of course, various systems of number and letter equivalents, and the wise individual will experiment, find which suits him or her best. As with any means of divination – tarot, *I Ching* or crystal ball – numerology is vital as a key to our Greater Consciousness, a tiny fraction of which is ever employed by most people.

The Hebrew alphabet is generally used by many – our illustration shows the number and letter equivalents. Numerologists reduce all the figures to one of the primal numbers, and to do this you merely add the numbers together until you reach a single digit.

Some, however, employ numbers as high as 11 and 12, believing these numbers represent a higher plane of experience. Eleven, they see, as the number for men and women with a strong sense of vocation – leaders such as statesman Sir Winston Churchill and

Right: **Sir Winston Churchill as a young man with his mother. Sir Winston is an 11 man: a number for those with a strong sense of vocation.**

reformer Florence Nightingale. Human relationships, they say, mean less to 11 people than their ideas. Einstein, for example, called himself a 'lone traveller', and what Picasso was told by his mother could apply to any of them in this bracket: 'If you become a soldier, you'll be a general. If you become a monk, you'll end up as the Pope.'

The Hebrew alphabet method of using letters of the alphabet in numerology.

Psychic Painter – *Barbara Hicken*

Next my Paranormal journey took me down to Torquay on the South Devon coast.

Back in the 1930s, traveller and writer Arthur Mee asked: 'Why go to the French Riviera as long as England has Torquay? Nature and man together have filled it with splendour, and it has glorious Devon all about it at the back of its beautiful bay.' Arthur Mee would see many changes today, but Torbay still retains a certain elegance.

A psychic painter had drawn me to Torquay on an early January morning, a day of cold winds and, later, driving spears of rain. A Pisces subject with brown eyes, Barbara Hicken was born in Manchester just over forty years ago. Formerly a waitress, she started painting in the mid 1970s. 'It was as if a big bright light was suddenly lit inside my head.' Most of her paintings are landscapes. She receives regular commissions and sells virtually every picture she paints.

But occasionally in Barbara Hicken's painting life somebody else – some power or some mystical presence – takes over.

The first portrait she painted under psychic influence was of the Queen back in 1983. It was purchased by a former member of the Royal Household who, in turn, presented it to Her Majesty.

'I was driven to do this painting... got obsessed by it. I then painted a portrait of the Queen Mother. Each time the need to undertake the painting has driven me crazy until it is on the canvas. *Then* I can sleep. When I begin it is as though I have the final product in my head.'

After completing her impressive study of the Queen Mother, Barbara Hicken met Romany clairvoyant Acora at his consulting room in Plymouth's Barbican.

'By this time I had started a third psychic painting, a portrait of Lord Louis Mountbatten. After I met Acora I put it on one side because I couldn't rest until I had painted him. It wasn't me doing it. His appearance came to me as if seen in a dream. Again, as when I painted the Queen, the room became very hot. As I worked on Acora's portrait Mountbatten's spirit tormented me and wouldn't let me go. He was fighting for me to return to his portrait and get it done. He was annoyed that I was doing this portrait and insisting that I must paint his right away. At one point he made me damage Acora's painting. He was jealous and just like a child trying to spoil it. I slashed across the painting with my brush – then I threw it down and cried like a child.'

Repairing the damage, she completed the portrait and presented it to Acora who now has it hanging in his shop.

'Acora's mother and grandmother were with me when I painted his gold rings. I did them in a flash. Odd things happened. The door creaked and vibrated although it was tightly shut on a ball catch and there was no draught. At another point I suddenly started laughing as I was doing the detail with a fine brush and it was then I damaged the painting. But I had to put Acora down on canvas. I had been dreaming about him every night.'

'Barbara,' I asked, 'what is this driving force that makes you do these psychic paintings?'

'I know it's not me,' she said. 'It comes from somewhere else... I've never actually seen anyone but there's something so powerful inside me that it's *not me* any more. My hand goes light. Normally my arms would ache if I held the brush too long in one position but at these times it's all done for me.'

'Are you quite sure Lord Louis Mountbatten or his spirit didn't want you to do that painting of Acora's?'

'Oh, definitely he didn't want me doing it. There was this funny stuff like smoke in the studio, although it wasn't smoke. I felt I was going to be ill. I ran out of the studio and phoned my husband. The other strange thing is that there were four eyes on the painting – another face on top of the canvas – it was like somebody fitting a cut out. Most peculiar.'

'Barbara, there is one thing I want to be clear about in my own mind. Is it true to say that you do two types of painting, one which, if I can use such words, is "ordinary painting", when you are, say, painting a landscape, and *then* there is another kind of painting when you would appear to be painting under some psychic influence?'

**Psychic painter Barbara Hicken with Acora
and her painting of the Romany clairvoyant
at The Barbican, Plymouth.**

'Yes,' she explained, 'with the portraits I know I'm being guided by some master painters of the past... Sir John Everatt Millais, Rembrandt and Hilliard, a Royal miniaturist who was born in 1547, all guide me.'

'In these portraits you've been drawn to the Royals. Some cynic might say: "Why doesn't she paint poor old Joe Bloggs living up on Dartmoor?" Is there a Royal connection in previous life?'

'There are several painters from the past who take me over,' Barbara replied. 'One, in particular, was a royal painter who wanted to paint the Queen but never finished that side of his work. Michael, can you believe me: I haven't got the choice... it's not me. Actually my very first portraits, 6 inch by 8 inch on panel, were Queen Elizabeth I and Henry VIII. I painted them out in great detail and then threw them away because it embarrassed me to see them! I know I was absolutely driven to paint them.'

**Barbara Hicken's painting of a Plymouth
Sound lighthouse, also painted under
psychic influence.**

That morning in Torquay, though, I especially liked a non-Royal painting of hers. A lighthouse, it had an eerie, almost Supernatural quality.

'That came to me in a dream,' she said, 'I love the sea, but I am frightened by the sea, and yet I have always wanted the excuse of being *in* a lighthouse... I was so tormented by this... I just *had* to paint it. In the dream I had been *there*, and a man, who goes out there to this lighthouse in Plymouth Sound, saw the painting and said: "Good God, it makes me feel as though I should get my boots on to go!"'

'Getting away from the portraits, looking at some of the photographs of your paintings in your files, there are some old country scenes, almost as if you've gone back in time. Do you time travel?'

'I was there,' she said, 'smelling the grass and the hay.'

'But do you think that was a memory or do you think you, in fact, travelled back *in time*?'

'I just *know* I was there.'

'Do you feel a different person when you're under these psychic influences?'

'Oh, yes. Absolutely. I feel a man. It's a man who's painting. So I act like a man, paint like a man, *and* talk like a man. Strange things happen when I'm painting. In one, I'd started to finish when all of a sudden a face came on to the painting. I hadn't put it there. So I painted it out. But it still came back.'

'And it wasn't you?'

'No, no. I would give my life if I could prove it.'

'What about the future?' I asked.

'Sir John Betjeman is trying to get me to paint him. He's been making contact from the other side.'

Not a Royal but, at least, the man appointed by the Queen to be Poet Laureate. Driving along Torquay seafront a little later, I remembered Acora had once been described as 'a prince among fortune tellers'. I remembered, too, he had been photographed alongside the ill-fated Lord Louis shortly before his assassination.

It is a strange fact, but Barbara Hicken seems to be haunted by Royalty.

Is there a link with a former Royal life? That question stayed with me all the way back to North Cornwall.

Medium – *John Graham*

John Graham is another psychic all-rounder.

Healer, clairvoyant and medium, he is a busy man. I was interested to hear about his work as a medium. It was, in fact, my first meeting with one, and he was something of a surprise. Bespectacled and bearded, in his open neck shirt and sweater, he looked – and sounded – a very down-to-earth character: not at all the mystic I had pictured in my mind's eye. Maybe I was thinking of those old photographs I had seen of Victorian mediums, men and women who had another-worldly look.

Anyway, he kindly agreed to meet me and restrict our conversation to 'contact with the other side'. It was a day 'lent', as we Cornish say, a November afternoon that might have been borrowed from September, when in places the low sunlight gave the landscape a diamond sharpness.

John Graham, his wife Margaret and their family live at Par: an end-of-terrace house in Par Lane called Journey's End. St Blaise, the patron saint of woolcombers, landed here in the third century. The Grahams moved from Leicester to Cornwall in 1984 and feel very happy at the edge of the sea in the china clay country. 'There is a great atmosphere in Cornwall, and now I wouldn't want to live anywhere else.'

Moreover, he believes Fate led them to this corner of Cornwall. 'I had this vision before we came down to Cornwall – originally we planned to settle in the Falmouth area – in which I was in a plane, looking down at the country. It was close to the sea, and I later

Right: **Medium John Graham: 'I just relax, open my mind and myself and let my feelings grow. Then I am contacted.'**

described it all to Margaret in considerable detail. Then, one day, when we were down in Cornwall house-hunting, I saw Par spread out from a road on the high ground and I realized I had been here before, though it was our first visit to Cornwall – I had seen it all in that vision.'

The high water of Spiritualism was a period from 1850 to 1890 when for four decades remarkable claims were made at séances, ranging from spirit materialization to levitation of the mediums, but once people, like the Psychical Research Society, began to impose stringent test conditions, these claims started to rapidly decrease. There is little doubt that in Victorian times some men and women were producing fake spirit phenomena for financial gain. Equally there have been mediums – sometimes called sensitives – who have been investigated by researchers and rated genuine: people like D. D. Home who demonstrated levitation – the rising and hovering in the air of objects or persons defying the laws of gravity – and was never caught cheating, or Mrs Osborne Leonard who convinced Sir Oliver Lodge of life after death.

John Graham readily admits that Spiritualism, at times, has had 'a bad press', and he was pleased to know I had asked for an interview because a mutual friend had said: 'You won't find a more sincere medium or man than John.'

He believes that Fate not only brought the family to Par, but to this house. 'We were planning to buy another property, and the whole thing fell through, and I felt very relieved. There I didn't feel right, but here there's a good atmosphere.'

I asked how he defined a medium.

'A person who is sensitive, who senses feelings *within* people.'

'How do you actually make contact with the other side? Is there any routine or special technique?'

'I just relax, open my mind and myself and let my feelings grow. Then I am contacted. Someone once said to me: "You talk to the dead." But they were wrong. They're not dead in the first place, and I don't talk to them, they talk to me.

'You've asked a difficult question because the contact comes in so many different ways. Sometimes I can be shown objects or symbols. You can see in what we call the third eye.'

He then went on to explain how he acts as an intermediary between the spirit world and this our everyday life.

'Whether it's a private sitting or a public meeting makes no difference. I pick up vibrations. If in the process I can bring these people closer together, then, yes, I do it, but it's entirely up to the person in spirit. I can't manufacture. Actually I'm suspicious of mediums who say they've made contact with Marilyn Monroe or the Duke of Windsor. This contact is a two-way thing, really three-way. You have the person at the sitting, wanting to make contact; you have the other person in spirit, and you have the medium in the middle.'

'What do you think happens,' I asked, 'when a person dies.'

'Well, the physical part, that's the bit left behind. The spirit or the soul, that's what goes on, that's the power. It's like a wireless set... it brings the power through it. That goes on... then back to the source of power whence it came. Everybody has got their own interpretation.'

I put another question, wondering if John Graham might think me an idiot this time.

'Won't some people think the other side a bit overcrowded?'

He chuckled and went on to explain that the other side isn't at all comparable with our material world. 'No, no.' he assured me, 'it won't be overcrowded. People have this idea of angels and trumpets in Heaven. There are millions and billions of forms over there.' We both agreed, in this world, man is limited, blinkered in fact.

Again I put a question which I thought might irritate him, but his reply showed great tolerance and understanding. 'How about film stars who have got through half-a-dozen marriages in their lives? What's going to happen in their hereafter?'

He chuckled again.

'Well, we'll revert back to that original power and a lot of these film stars, who have gone through half-a-dozen marriages have learnt a lot in life and yet, at the same time, they haven't learnt enough... and if they haven't learnt enough they'll come back in another form to learn a bit more in future.'

I then asked what would have happened to somebody as evil as Hitler.

'I feel Hitler has already had several incarnations,' he replied, 'and he will face many more until he learns the lessons needed to progress on a spiritual level.'

John Graham says he has had 'glimpses of life on the other side, but I suspect we are not meant to be too aware as there might be a tendency to opt out of our present life. When these glimpses take place, the one thing of paramount importance is the immeasurable peace. There's nothing comparable on our plane.'

'You're a disciple of reincarnation then?'

'I wouldn't say a disciple. I think it's a law of Nature. That's the process through which we grow. Reincarnation has the biggest possibility for everyone.'

'What about ghosts? Why do you think they reappear? Is it that they have not settled in the other life and are wanting to come back?'

There were a few moments silence before he replied this time.

'The majority have got something they haven't settled in *this* life. They have possibly gone very suddenly without completing something. They may even have taken their life and have now realized they've got something to complete, something they've not done. Tormented souls: there are various reasons why they keep coming back to try and complete what they haven't done earlier.'

'When you're contacting people who have departed this life, are you able to pick them up clearly in terms of either seeing or hearing them?'

'That depends on the person,' John Graham explained, 'who is in spirit *and* the person attending the sitting. You'd be amazed when you start getting the truth sometimes. The individual present will try and shut it off because they might have something which they don't want anyone to know. What they don't realize is that I would never open anything out in public which could be harmful to them or embarrass them.

'It is amazing once you start the truth coming out. Some people do shut down and that makes it difficult work for the medium. You get conflict in emotions. You get those on one side saying "that's right" and the other saying the reverse. Sometimes it's a voice in the mind. Sometimes it's feelings, impressions. The message can come in various ways, and on many occassions I have *seen* a figure from the other side.'

'And how do you see them,' I asked. 'Are they in their earthly form? Do you see them as they were in their heyday or in the last days of their earthly life?'

'It's entirely up to them,' the medium further explained, 'how they present themselves. Yes, to use a sporting term, "the ball is in their court". Sometimes they appear as vague, misty forms. It depends on how they want to come. Sometimes they come as clearly as you appear in the room this afternoon. I may be doing a public demonstration and I'm describing this person, but someone in the congregation can't quite figure out who it is, and suddenly the features or the appearance of the person in spirit will change. It's as if they're saying, "This is how *you* remember me." They may not have seen each other for years and years.

'I find that nowadays the younger generation especially are searching, more so than the older, but I believe a lot of damage is done by fakes and pretenders. In London I've sat at meetings where the so-called medium on the platform has made me shudder. I intuitively know when something is not right, and on the way home my wife will say "You were very quiet tonight!"

'I'm not saying that mediums and clairvoyants can't make mistakes. That's a human failing. We misinterpret what we have been given...

'I was brought up, well brought up in the Spiritualist Church, and, at one time, I helped to run a Spiritualist Church, but I don't like the name "Spiritualist".'

'If you had to fill in your passport on the other side, what would be your label?' I asked.

'Just a believer in Life. I don't class it as religion. I see it as a way of Life.'

'You don't subscribe to the view that the Lord's in Heaven until next Sunday at eleven.'

'No, no, and you don't need a church to be a Christian. You don't need a building to practise what you believe in. Yes, it's nice to sometimes get together in a church... people on the same vibration... but it isn't *necessary*. I've been to a number of different churches of different denominations... I feel you must keep on searching, must keep on asking questions. The pomp and ceremony of many church services leave me cold. There is no warmth.

'Often it's difficult for an educated person to accept the spiritual side. Often the more educated get less from life. It's interesting that some of the best mediums, some of the best clairvoyants come from the third world. It's what is *in* a person and not what's *around* them... this ability to receive the natural, the spiritual. I can pick up a presence in a house or a room or even in the open. We are all basically spirit. Everyone has the ability to be a medium to a certain degree, but it's more obvious in some of us... and it's hard work.'

Great Ley Line of the West

In England they are called old straight lines. In Ireland they become fairy lines. Across the Atlantic they are known as serpent power by the old Indian tribes. Down under in Australia the aborigines call them lines of song and in China they are referred to as dragon currents.

It was only sixty years ago or thereabouts in Britain that an English beer salesman visualized a web of lines 'linking holy places and sites of antiquity'.

Students of the Occult believe the ley line system signifies healing and renewal of the life force. They also believe emanations given off by the lines vary with different phases of the moon.

Locating ley-line energy was one of the oldest arts known to man, a properly taught science using divining rods.

Here in the Westcountry we have one of the truly great ley lines. Beginning at St Michael's Mount down in the foot of Cornwall, it goes on to the Cheesewring on Bodmin Moor, comes through to St Michael's Church at Brentor on the edge of Dartmoor, and on to Somerset to Burrow Mump and Glastonbury. Even then its journey does not end, for the line proceeds out of the region on to Avebury in Wiltshire; further eastward it follows the approximate course of the Icknield Way, through Bury St Edmunds and finally crossing the coast north of Lowestoft. Or is it finally?

Fact is when we travel these ley lines we find ourselves in an area of intriguing speculation and possibility.

For the purposes of this journey, we will restrict ourselves to the section of the ley beginning at the Mount and ending at Glastonbury.

Right: '**... the Mount remains a magical place.**'

It was not until the early 1920s that an amateur archaeologist, when studying maps, made a discovery. Alfred Watkins perceptively noted that prehistoric remains, together with many churches dating from the pre-reformation period, fell into alignments. Fieldwork confirmed his belief and he called such lines 'leys'. The basis of the ley system is very simple – that sites of ancient importance align.

More and more people have become convinced these leys are psychic power lines.

Dr Joseph Heinsch, a celebrated German ley hunter, for example, discovered that numerous ancient sites of pagan ceremony and old trackways appeared to link up geometrically. The Doctor reckoned that Holy lines radiated out from the hills, and churches were built along these lines because of a powerful spiritual something.

Certainly the ley hunter, who plots spiritual patterns across the landscape, is on a mystical quest for communion with Mother Earth. As we, twentieth-century searchers, walk these ancient trackways, the spirit of an ancient people and culture somehow touches us. The German Doctor was quite sure this culture was widespread over the planet long, long ago and further believed that modern science will in time uncover these long lost secrets – an exciting prospect.

Here is Rosemary Clinch writing on the subject in her chapter 'Strange Sightings & Mystical Paths' which appeared in *Strange Somerset Stories*, published by Bossiney in 1984:

'There is no overwhelming proof for the reasons why circles, tumuli and churches connect but the evidence is they do and it is hard to understand the reluctance of archaeologists to accept this. Anyone can prove it to themselves with a good, straight ruler, well-sharpened pencil and an ordnance survey map.

'Just simply look for an ancient site, tump, cairn or fort. Look for other similar sites including churches, Roman forts, beacon points or holy wells. Crossroads, ancient castles, islands and ponds are all likely candidates – ring them all before taking the ruler to see if any of them connect.

'It is surprising what one can learn about the countryside if prepared to run the risk of being called a "dotty archaeologist"!

'Megalithic Man's reshaping of our landscape with his movement of stones has a lot to answer for. Maybe we know how he dragged the Bluestones for Stonehenge from Prescelly but we still strive to understand his mind and his motives. Maybe legends and folklore have the answers, intangible though they may be, and perhaps there is more to be learned from the ancient art of dowsing.

'The achievements of man 5,000 years ago, were strange enough to have warranted the use of forces beyond the knowledge of man today and it can only remain to be said. "There are more things in heaven and earth..." '

Let us then go down to West Cornwall, to St Michael's Mount: a romantic island castle set in beautiful Mount's Bay. Castles inevitably are woven into the Arthurian tapestry, interestingly our ley line journey begins *and* ends with the great King.

This is Tennyson's imagined isle:
And we came to the Isle of Flowers,
Their breath met us out on the sea,
For the Spring and the middle Summer
Sat each on the lap of the breeze.

How the Mount got its name is a question of choice. There are a brace of theories. One says St Michael himself once appeared in a vision to a hermit on the Mount, a Supernatural happening which fired Milton to produce *The great vision of the guarded mount*. The second version is that St Michael appeared in another vision to a group of Cornish fishermen who saw him standing on a rock on the island in the year 495 which, of course, takes us back to Arthur's time.

Either way, the Mount remains a magical place. Ann Treneer, one of our best native Cornish writers, saw it 'on a winter morning, when the sun is low... in a wash of silver'. Young Humphry Davy cared for it most by moonlight.

I last came to Marazion on a brilliant October morning when sunlight intensified everything on land and in the sky. That morning I sensed no better place to begin a quest for the Holy Grail.

Our second destination along the ley is the Cheesewring high on the eastern flank of Bodmin Moor. Standing in front of the Cheesewring, you begin to understand Nature is no less than a genius in sculpture. It has the appearance of being man-made, the stones balancing beautifully on the western side of Stowe Hill, but the belief is it's a natural formation. From certain angles, too, you are reminded of the sculpture of the dynamic Dame Barbara Hepworth.

In *The Moors of Cornwall* I have written: 'Try and come here on a crystal-clear day and you will be richly rewarded. From these grey-blue stones whole chunks of both Cornwall and Devon are visible: the English Channel to the south and the Atlantic to the north. Eastward sprawls Dartmoor and if you are really lucky Exmoor too can be seen.

'From such a pinnacle you get a definite feel of the Moor: the grey granite scattered across the brown and the greens of the landscape.'

The old folk believed such stones were the remains of a huge interconnected power temple – Bowerman's Nose on Dartmoor is a kindred spirit. They believed the Cornish temples were dedicated to the wellbeing of the body whereas their Devon counterparts were for revitalizing the spirit. All I know is that I feel better for coming here.

On the third stage of the journey along the ley we come to St Michael's Church at Brent Tor. 37 feet long and 14 feet 6 inches wide, it is the fourth smallest parish church in the kingdom. It stands 1008 feet above sea level. There is no road for a car. Brides have to walk every inch of the steep slope.

Some old buildings speak to us – that is provided we have the humility to be quiet and listen. St Michael's – for me – has the ability to refresh, renew. The pamphlet in the church probably gives us a clue:

Are you a Christian? Do you believe?
If you are, then stop. Draw near to God. Pray for us and yourself.
If you are not, we hope that you may stay for a while in this hallowed building where you may discover something of God's majesty and the nearness of his presence.
So please don't hurry away.

Here at Brent Tor I agree with those searchers who say these ley lines carry energy flows. A visit here is always a worthwhile experience, a renewing of the batteries.

Our knowledge of earth energy culture basically comes from China where the art of divining the earth energies, flowing along the leys – 'dragon paths' the Chinese call them – enabled people to

Left: **The Cheesewring high on the eastern flank of Bodmin Moor.**

decide where best to build a house or temple: a spot which would harmonise with the flow of energy from the earth. It is interesting that when Rudyard Kipling, who spent many years in the East, made his first visit to Batemans, his seventeenth-century house in Sussex, he reacted positively: 'We entered and found her spirit, her *feng shui* – to be good.'

At Brent Tor I know precisely what Mr Kipling meant. Here too the spirit is 'good'.

Our ley now takes us on to Somerset: to Burrow Mump, Burrow Bridge. Here a large mound, partly and maybe completely artificial, is topped by ruins – the remains of a church dedicated to the same Saint: St Michael.

Places like this make you think back to Alfred Watkins, aged 65, riding on horseback across the hills near Bredwardine. He pulled up his horse to look across at the countryside spread out below and, in one brilliant, inspired moment, he became aware of a 'network of lines, standing out like glowing wires all over the surface of the country, intersecting at the sites of churches, old stones and other spots of traditional sanctity'.

From that moment for many of us a new light was lit on the landscape and in Life itself.

From this Somerset mound we proceed to Glastonbury. Now we come to one of the most magical spots in the whole Westcountry. As St Michael's Mount was a perfect starting point for our ley line journey, so Glastonbury is a fitting climax.

Sally Jones in her well-crafted *Mysteries in the Somerset Landscape* has written: 'Glastonbury has always acted like a magnet, not just for gypsies but for everyone, pagan or Christian, seeking clues to the deep mysteries of life and the after-life. The strange conical hill has another-worldly quality, rearing as it does high and steep-sided out of the Isle of Avalon surrounded by level acres.

'With its long narrow base beneath the ridged hump, it reminds me irresistibly of a tall green ship setting out on a journey to an unknown country, an impression reinforced by the curious spiral tracks winding round the hill, reminiscent of rolling grassy waves. To many, these tracks are proof of the Tor's supernatural origin so

Left: **St Michael's Church at Brent Tor: 'It stands 1,008 feet above sea level.'**

it is a surprise to learn that they are in fact natural and common to several of the other tors and hillocks dotted about Somerset.'

In earlier researches, I interviewed a member of a Westcountry psycho-expansion group who claims to have been King Arthur in an earlier life. In addition to confirming that he had been here, 'Arthur' was able to tell me the tor has changed substantially. There was, according to my informant, once a temple on the summit, circular, Greek like, with a beautiful mosaic type floor.

The tor undoubtedly works on different people in different ways. Author Colin Wilson told me that when he walks up Glastonbury Tor, with a dowsing rod in his hands, 'it twists up and down with a strength and persistence that makes my fingers tired. My wife, who is a far better dowser than I am, found that the "field" of the Tor made her feel sick.'

Early man believed the Universe to be magical and the Earth a living creature. Those primitive people were almost certainly the pioneer dowsers, responding naturally to the earth's forces.

Tom Lethbridge, who had strong links with the Westcountry, and by the time he died was being called 'the Einstein of the Paranormal', was convinced Nature is full of strange 'tape recordings' that possibly date back millions of years.

My personal interest in ley lines has deepened for the simple reason that I invariably experience a heightened sense of wellbeing at most places on these lines – rather as in the case with spiritual healing.

As far as Somerset is concerned, perhaps then the last words should come from thoughtful, perceptive Sally Jones. Writing on the mysteries of Somerset, she reflected: 'Once you become immersed in them and begin to explore the landscapes in which they are rooted, the impossible is suddenly possible and the magical is transformed into just another dimension of reality.'

Left: **Glastonbury Tor – '... one of the most magical spots in the Westcountry.'**

Healer of Animals & Human Beings –
Nelson Side

Nelson Side is a kind of legend in the countryside of Cornwall.

He is a healer with a difference – many of his patients are four-legged: some are domestic pets, but the great majority are livestock belonging to the farms and smallholdings in this northern corner of Cornwall.

We talked at his home in Camelford on a cold February evening, when the wind whistled through the narrow streets of the town – which some say is the Camelot of King Arthur fame. Nelson Side was born in Camelford more than seventy years ago and has lived here all his life, apart from his war years in the army. He looks and moves like a man, at least, ten years younger. A retired postman, with grey blue eyes, you are immediately aware of the fact that you are in the presence of no ordinary ex-postman – though he loved every day of his working life in post-office uniform.

His whole lifestyle changed in his forties, when suddenly he discovered he possessed the power to heal.

From then on, he has devoted hundreds of hours to healing sick people and sick animals – yet he never takes any money for all his time and effort. He is that very rare individual: a man who has steadfastly declined to make money out of his gift.

'If I took money, I feel I might lose the gift,' he told me. 'It all began when I went to a lady's house with the mail one morning, and when she answered the door, she was wearing a bandage around her leg. I just asked: "What happened?" "Oh," she said, "I was playing badminton last night and I stepped back to retrieve a flight and pulled a cord." I don't know what made me say it, but I said: "I think I can help you."'

Left: **Nelson Side – healer with a difference.**
Many of his patients are four-legged.

'So I just lay my hands on her, and said "You can take off that bandage. I'll pop in tomorrow to see if the swelling's gone." I went in the next day and she said: "It's fine!"'

'Healing came out of the blue like that, though, you see, my dad had an inkling toward this, but he wasn't so strong as I am. Of course, the more you do, the stronger you become.

'Actually I prefer to deal with animals rather than human beings. Some people can't relax, and that makes it very difficult for the healer. With some people I can do next to nothing, but when we're one, when we're both relaxed, that's the time when I get to work. I can feel it in my hands, whether I can do any good or not.'

He stretched out his hands.

'I don't want faith or anything like that. I'm not a faith healer. I don't perform or go through any ritual. The first thing I go for is the inflammation. No matter what the problem is, there is no pain in the body without inflammation. I can remove the inflammation and by doing so the pain goes after a while... and that's the time they begin to feel OK.

'If you sprain your wrist or your ankle or anything like that and you can't put your foot to the ground, then in twenty minutes I'd have you walking. It can be pretty rapid. I cannot do anything as regards the bruising or the swelling, but I can tell you that you'll walk in the morning without pain. I warn everyone, though, that within about six hours a pain will return. It can be severe but it only lasts a short time and I can say, "Forget it because you'll be all right in the morning." '

In the early years, Nelson Side was reluctant to publicise his health work. He remains the most modest of men, but it was a horse which introduced him to a wider public.

'They brought me in at Tall Trees, the riding stables at Davidstow,' he explained, 'and Mrs Harrison, who runs the stables, asked me to come up there to see this horse. She told me what the vet had said, so I said, "I can't do any harm; so I'll have a go."

'I put my hands on the horse and found the spot where the inflammation was... I found the inflammation and could see there was no reason why the horse shouldn't be right. I don't ask for progress reports. If there's no news that means it's good news. I only hear from people again if they or the animal need more help. Well, about a fortnight later Mrs Harrison rang up to say the local paper wanted to interview and photograph me. She had been there with me at the stables when I had worked on the horse and had told the newspaper all about it.

'I didn't want the publicity, but they said it was too good a story, and that half-page story and photograph in the paper opened the door to a great many more animals and people.

'Yesterday afternoon I was out with sheep at a farm near Launceston, a case of swallow eye, a kind of blindness, a film that comes across the eyes of the sheep. I saw about twenty sheep up there. With sheep or cattle, say a herd suffering from ringworm, I often just walk among them.'

'And that works – by simply walking among them?'

'Oh, yes, it works. I cured about fifty sheep on the same farm last year, all suffering from swallow eye. Eyes are an important sign. If an animal is in pain, the eyes are dull and sunken, but if the eyes are bright that's a good sign, and the same is true of people as well.

'I've even cured cattle of ringworm by telling the farmer to walk among his cattle, thinking of me, and picturing me in his mind. By visualizing me, he has been able to do the healing, but I find this works only once. If he asks a second time then I have to go back to the farm and see the animals for myself.'

Despite illness in the family, Nelson himself has not been to a doctor for more than forty years. He attributes his healthy lifestyle to basically three things: a very contented life – he really enjoyed his work as a postman and now he is happy and purposeful in his work as a healer – his wife's good cooking and the fact that he gave up smoking. 'I started smoking at the age of ten, and gave it up at forty!'

I asked him how his healing, his laying on of hands works.

'Honestly, I don't know,' he said. 'I can't begin to tell you or explain, but within minutes of putting my hand on a person or an animal, if the inflammation is bad, then I feel it in my hands. It's as if my hands are in a bunch of stinging nettles.

'Oh, yes, I have this reaction. You see I can only do so much healing because it takes so much out of me. I feel as if something's gone. I draw out the inflammation and hold *that*, and it takes me about three-quarters of an hour, maybe sometimes longer, to get that gone. So if I worked on you for half an hour, I wouldn't be able to work on another person for about an hour and a half. That's how it works, and that's why I have to see only about three people a day.

'I'm the channel. I have had this gift given to me by someone, unknown, and I can heal through that gift. That's just what it amounts to, but how it's done, I don't know... I can't put it into words but I know it works.

'I'll give you an instance. It was last year and I was called to this farm; they had a Hereford heifer, only fourteen or fifteen months old. A nice heifer, but it was carrying its leg. I bent down and it was all inflamed, all swollen up. I could feel the heat. But the animal was mine. I could do anything with it. Animals *know* when you're tying to help them. The farmer said: "Do you think it's sprained?" I said: "No, it looks like poison." Anyway I worked on the heifer, and when I came home I was sitting down in the chair and suddenly said to my wife: "That heifer's been bitten by an adder!"

'Next day, I went back to the farm, and worked on the animal again and looked for the puncture. I couldn't find one, but three days later I made a visit and it had just started to discharge through the puncture where it was bitten, with the swelling almost gone. Then after another three days, the farmer phoned me again and I

'... Nelson Side is probably closest to God healing cattle in the countryside.'

went back – it had started swelling again. I said: "This animal was bitten twice, and it'll connect where it was punctured above", and sure enough it did. Now that animal is perfect. But the vets would have put it down.'

'How do you and the veterinary surgeons get on?' I asked.

'Well, some are all right,' said Nelson with a smile, 'but others are scathing. They don't believe in it, but I can do something they can't do. I take out the inflammation and one vet agreed with me when I said that to him.'

Brought up in the Methodist chapel tradition, he recalls: 'I loved Bible reading as a child. I still believe in Christianity and believe in God, but nowadays I rarely go to chapel... it's usually a wedding or a funeral.'

You get the impression Nelson Side is probably closest to God healing cattle in the countryside or working on a sick person by his fireside. He also believes in the importance of enjoying 'the here and now'. It is hard to imagine him wasting an hour – or being bored. 'Tomorrow I have three people coming to see me at different stages in the day. Then on Thursday I have to go to Bodmin and on Friday a lady is coming all the way from St Merryn to see me. She's been coming to see me for two years and is almost cured now.

'I know when I'm helping someone. I know in a moment. I can visualize the whole human body and I see the spot where the trouble is. With animals I don't always need to be there. I can visualize very clear pictures of animals, but with human beings I need to be with them.

'Funny thing happened to me a while back. A farmer phoned and said: 'Ten of my cattle have ringworm.' I told him to walk among the cattle, thinking of me. When I next saw him, he said: 'All the cattle were cleared of that ringworm except one... I'd miscounted. There were eleven not ten...'

Nelson is a great believer in 'hot olive oil and starch. Those were old mother's remedies.' He makes no rash promises, but is prepared to tackle any condition. 'I'm not afraid to put my hand on a troubled part of the body, but not on a dog. I was bitten twice by dogs and it destroyed my confidence for a while. Dogs apart, I'm prepared to have a go at anything. A few months ago, I had a man come in with pleurisy. He ought to have been home in bed. Anyway I worked on him and within twenty minutes, he was taking deep breaths, something he hadn't done for four days.

'Another case I had was an elderly lady who had fallen downstairs, and I worked on her. The next morning, when I called on her, she said, "What have you done to me – look." She was walking normally.

'I can generate heat. I once put a cow to sleep and more than once I've had somebody pass out when I've been working on them!

'I can run my hands down a spine and *find* the spot, the trapped nerve, and in that moment I feel *the shiver* go right over me.

'Healing can help depression. Now it's a funny thing. Though depression is in the head, I pull it out of the head first and then the feet. I use both hands often, pushing with the right hand and pulling with the left and visualizing all the time. And at the end of it, I feel elated, a little weary perhaps, but on top of the world.'

In Search of Proof

As I implied earlier, words like evidence and proof are difficult enough at the best of times, and in a Paranormal context they become more so. Or do they?

Anyway at this late stage on our journey, I decided to piece together some claims. Independently, some of them may appear to be slightly lightweight, but collectively I believe they represent a solid body of evidence, a fascinating catalogue in fact.

One of the first people I interviewed in the Paranormal field was Betty Lukey, a very talented clairvoyant and articulate lady. She had no doubt whatsoever that the thing we call death is not the end, but the beginning of another stage. First, she told me how she had ten friends in for a table-turning session, and with her husband Lewis, it made a party of twelve.

'We sat round a table' she said, 'with the letters of the alphabet set in a circle, in the centre of which was a glass tumbler turned upside down; we each rested a tip of a finger on the glass, sat in silence and awaited results having asked, "Is anybody there?" After a while the glass began to move, and various messages were spelt out. At this stage, my Finnish maid, Margot, peered through a portion of the stained-glass window in the upper part of the door to see if we were ready for coffee and sandwiches. I had specifically said, "Don't come into the room until the lights are on!" She saw an old man sitting on the arm of a chair, in which a woman sat. Then Margot counted and found it came to thirteen people, so she placed another plate, cup and saucer on the trolley.'

Later, that evening after the guests had gone, Betty questioned Margot closely about 'the old man' and the girl gave a very detailed description of the gentleman – so detailed that Betty 'recognised' him as the father of the woman who had been sitting in the chair. Moreover, she knew he had been dead for as long as three years.

Betty Lukey had another particularly vivid experience – this time relating to her father, Frederick Rowley Lake, a director of Hawker, the well-known Westcountry wine merchants. Mr Lake was a disbeliever, and Betty was so keen to convince him there was another life and a whole psychic field that they made a pact. Daughter said to father: 'In view of your disbelief, I'll come and haunt you if I go first. I'll come and blow you a kiss! But if you go first, you must come and see me... and let me see and smell that old Harris Tweed jacket you should have thrown away years ago.' It was a year after his death – I was then living at Crantock – and I came across him sleeping in a deckchair. He was wearing his old Harris Tweed jacket, his glasses had fallen on his lap and his panama hat had slipped forward... just as he'd been when with me at Crantock two years before.'

Supernatural smells are rare. But one man, who has experienced them, is healer and Spiritualist Alan Nance – again it concerns a late father. He told me: 'There was an interesting point about my father's death. He had a great love of toast, and after he had passed over, the whole house was permeated with the smell of toast. The smell of toast even followed me to Australia... distance doesn't deter the spirit world.'

Some time ago Alan showed me an extract from *Man and the Spiritual World* by the Reverend Arthur Chambers, something published at the turn of the century. Taking the form of a reported seance, it tells the story of a not particularly well-educated young Englishman acting as the medium, and how under trance he was capable of speaking fluently in Hindustani.

'Isn't that stretching our credibility a bit too far?' I probed. Alan laughed: 'Not a bit of it. I heard a French medium, in a trance state, speak cut-glass English which she never used in her normal Australian conversation! She was a French woman living down under.'

Alan Nance believes the evidence for Life after death is overwhelming. 'Thousands and thousands of messages have been received from the other side,' he says. 'All those people can't be under some grand delusion.'

After the publication of my *Strange Happenings in Cornwall,* in 1981, I had an interesting letter from Mrs P. Williams (no relation) of Plymstock, Devon, telling me about her strange Cornish happening, some years ago at Cape Cornwall.

'We set out from Madron on a lovely sunny day in August,' she

**Betty Lukey, a very talented clairvoyant.
She had no doubt whatsoever that the thing
we call death is not the end...**

wrote. 'Cape Cornwall was bathed in sunshine, the sky a glorious blue and the sea a sheet of blue with silver ripples. All was well until suddenly a sinister black cloud appeared overhead, and the green, springy turf underfoot became an area of scorched earth and we were enveloped in a cloud of malignant unseen witnesses... clad in armour... and the noise of battle.

'We fled in haste from the savage scene to the security of green turf and blue sky which strangely enough looked as if nothing had changed. Though in no way given to flights of fancy, my late

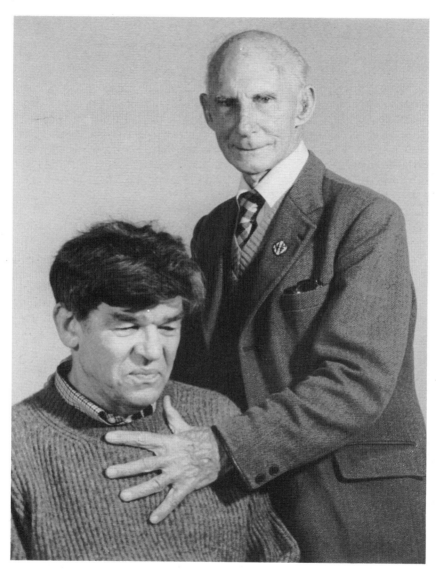

Healer Alan Nance: 'I heard a French medium, in a tranced state, speak cut-glass English which she never used in her normal Australian conversation!'

husband was as shaken as I. We did not repeat the journey. One encounter with the spirit world being quite enough!'

Strangely enough, soon after getting that letter from Mrs Williams, Colin Wilson in a manuscript to Bossiney related the strange experience of Stephen Jenkins near Mount's Bay in West Cornwall. Suddenly Stephen Jenkins thought he was suffering from an optical illusion. Immediately ahead among clumps and bushes was a contingent of armed men. He began to run towards them, and at once 'something like a curtain of heated air wavered in front of them briefly – and there were only bushes and stones...' Colin Wilson believes the young man was picking up something from the past – the scene of a battle perhaps.

Turning to the field of healing, here we can find literally hundreds, probably thousands of people in the Westcountry who have derived benefit from healing.

Pat Dennis, a Bossiney colleague, who introduced me to Nelson Side of Camelford, has received healing from both Nelson and Barney Camfield. Pat has no doubt she has been helped by both. In a recent case of severe back ache, she found a single visit to Nelson immediately generated heat and a sense of peace and, most significantly, on that very night she experienced no pain: the first time in several weeks she had been free of pain.

Later I asked Pat's farmer husband Derek how he rated Nelson Side.

'Nelson's a master chap,' said Derek. 'I badly sprained an ankle getting sheep in for shearing, and I went to see Nelson. He took the inflammation out right away and next day I was walking and working. He helped me, too, when I had ulcer trouble. You feel this tremendous heat like an electric heater from the palm of his hand, and he's done wonderful things with our cattle and sheep.'

Readers of Barney Camfield's book *Healing, Harmony & Health* will find many examples of people deriving benefit from healing, and often such people only go to a healer as a very last resort. Here is something he wrote in his first chapter called 'What is a "Healer?"':

'One such case comes to mind in connection with a television programme I had been asked to take part in. Dr Alec Forbes had asked me to give healing to a patient while linked to a battery powered electro-encephalograph. The patient would also be connected to a separate machine, both of which would show our individual brainwaves. Healers are supposed to have a strong "alpha" wave and also experiments have shown that when healing is given the patient's brainwaves tend to change and match the healer's pattern of waves.

'I asked the producer of the programme if they could find the patient themselves, preferably someone who had never received healing treatment from me or anyone else. I did not want it thought that there had been any kind of influence. They apparently got in touch with the Arthritis & Rheumatism Council and a volunteer, Norah, appeared at the studio shortly before the programme was due to be taped.

'Geoffrey Blundell arrived from London with his two machines, much too late for there to be any trial of the machines. In fact, they were still being set up after the start of the show during the running of a film. But the demonstration worked. Yes, my "alpha" rhythm was strong. And it and the other brain rhythms were quite different from those of the patient. I stood behind her and gave her healing and within a couple of minutes her brainwaves changed and began to match mine. Upon being questioned, she said that she felt a lovely comfortable glow!

'I had warned her that she would most probably feel extra pain the following day, but what I hadn't thought about too much was just how long the period of healing was going to be! I don't give arthritics too long on the first run because I don't want the patient to suffer too much. I try to get them used to it slowly, but on this occasion we couldn't move while Alec Forbes, the interviewer and Geoffrey Blundell were discussing healing and brainwaves, the machines and goodness knows what. And I couldn't turn it off! The healing I mean.

'Poor Norah. She told me later that week that the following day she was in such pain that she spent the day in bed. And wished then that she had never met me! But the following day she felt fine. No arthritic pain; and she hasn't suffered from it since she told me. And that was six years ago.'

In the light of experiences of that nature, I now veer strongly to the view that limits exist only in our minds.

Also Available

PEOPLE AND PLACES IN CORNWALL
by Michael Williams
Featuring Sir John Betjeman, Marika Hanbury Tenison, Barbara Hepworth and seven other characters, all of whom contributed richly to the Cornish scene.
'... outlines ten notable characters ... whose lives and work have been influenced by "Cornwall's genius to fire creativity"... a fascinating study.'
The Cornish Guardian

MYSTERIES IN THE DEVON LANDSCAPE
by Hilary Wreford & Michael Williams
Outstanding photographs and illuminating text about eerie aspects of Devon. Seen on TSW and Channel 4. Author interviews on DevonAir and BBC Radio Devon.
'... a fascinating book. But it is worth getting just for the superb pictures...'
Express & Echo

OCCULT IN THE WEST
by Michael Williams. Over 30 photographs.
Michael Williams follows his successful Supernatural in Cornwall with further interviews and investigations into the Occult – this time incorporating Devon. Ghosts and clairvoyancy, dreams and psychic painting, healing and hypnosis are only some of the facets of a fascinating story.
'... provides the doubters with much food for thought.'
Jean Kenzie, Tavistock Gazette

STRANGE SOMERSET STORIES
Introduced by David Foot with chapters by Ray Waddon, Jack Hurley, Lornie Leete-Hodge, Hilary Wreford, David Foot, Rosemary Clinch and Michael Williams.
'... a good collection of yarns about Somerset's eccentrics, weird legends and architectural follies...'
Dan Lees, The Western Daily Press

CURIOSITIES OF SOMERSET
by Lornie Leete-Hodge
A look at some of the unusual and sometimes strange aspects of Somerset.
'Words and pictures combine to capture that unique quality that is Somerset.'
Western Gazette

GHOSTS OF SOMERSET
by Peter Underwood
The President of the Ghost Club completes a hat-trick of hauntings for Bossiney.
'... many spirits that have sent shivers down the spines over the years...'
Somerset County Gazette

WESTCOUNTRY MYSTERIES
Introduced by Colin Wilson
A team of authors probe mysterious happenings in Somerset, Devon and Cornwall. Drawings and photographs all add to the mysterious content.
'... strange goings-on in Britain's south-west peninsula... recommended.'
Doc Shiels, Fortean Times

HEALING, HARMONY & HEALTH

by Barney Camfield

Healing in its various forms, the significance of handwriting and dreams, and psycho-expansion.

'If you are tuned in to the right wave length of new age thinking... you won't want to put it down until you get to the last page.'

David Rose, Western Evening Herald

THE MOORS OF CORNWALL

by Michael Williams

Contains 77 photographs and drawings. The first ever publication to incorporate the three main moorland areas of Cornwall.

'... is not only a celebration in words of the Moors and their ancient pagan stones and granite strewn tors but a remarkable collection of photographs and drawings of Penwith, Goss and Bodmin Moors...'

Sarah Foot, The Editor, Cornish Scene

COASTLINE OF CORNWALL

by Ken Duxbury

Ken Duxbury has spent thirty years sailing the seas of Cornwall, walking its clifftops, exploring its caves and beaches, using its harbours and creeks.

'... a trip in words and pictures from Hawker's Morwenstow in the north, round Land's End and the Lizard to the gentle slopes of Mount Edgcumbe country park.'

The Western Morning News

AROUND LAND'S END

Michael Williams explores the end and the beginning of Cornwall. Wrecks and legends, the Minack Theatre, Cable & Wireless, Penwith characters and customs, lighthouses and Lyonesse all feature. 90 photographs, many of them from Edwardian and Victorian times, help to tell the story.

'... a delightful stroll not only along the lanes but the legends of this celebrated area.'

The Cornishman

UNKNOWN CORNWALL

by Michael Williams

84 drawings and photographs nearly all especially commissioned for this publication, portraying features of Cornwall rarely seen on the published page.

'... a treasure chest of rich jewels that will surprise many people who pride themselves on a thorough knowledge ...'

Western Evening Herald

SUPERSTITION AND FOLKLORE

by Michael Williams. 44 photographs.

A survey of Westcountry Superstitions: Interviews on the subject and some Cornish and Devon folklore.

'... the strictures that we all ignore at our peril. To help us to keep out of trouble, Mr Williams has prepared a comprehensive list.'

Frank Kempe, North Devon Journal-Herald

We shall be pleased to send you our catalogue giving full details of our growing list of titles for Devon, Cornwall and Somerset and forthcoming publications.

If you have difficulty in obtaining our titles, write direct to Bossiney Books, Land's End, St Teath, Bodmin, Cornwall.